Young Mothers' Voices

An Anthology by

the Young Women of

The Chiles Academy

Daytona Beach, Florida

Compiled, edited and published by:

Armstrong Media Group, LLC

Uppity Women Press

i

Young Mother's Voices – an Anthology

Copyright ©2016 by Armstrong Media Group, LLC and
Uppity Woman Press

ISBN# 978-0692712597

#10-0692712593

Cover art by Chris Holmes at whiterabbitgraphix.com

Table of Contents

Introduction
Glenda Taylor

This anthology is a collection of voices that belie many faulty societal representations of pregnant and parenting teens. The young mothers at The Chiles Academy are proving daily that stereotypes of teenage mothers do not define them. Discovering who they are, is for them, as it is for all of us, a work in progress.

The staff, teachers and volunteers of this school are privileged and sometimes challenged to listen to the voices of these students. We listen as they talk about books they are reading, as they risk developing new relationships while they mourn others, and as they learn to celebrate the uniqueness of themselves and their children. Their voices as writers reveal that they each have a deep well from which to draw.

This collection of poems, personal narratives, letters and stories give voice to the pain, anger, joy and creativity of young mothers, as they share who they are and who they are becoming. We hope that you will hear them as we do, each a unique song... each so worth knowing.

Special thanks to the following who were instrumental in making this anthology possible: Mr. Mike Pyle of Armstrong Media Group and Mrs. Veronica H. Hart of Uppity Woman Press, our editors and publishers, who helped make a dream come true; the English teachers who taught and supported the writing of our students; Ms. Lute, Mrs. Hope, and Mrs. Hall; Ms. Sheryl Bell whose relentless encouragement of students, faculty and volunteers kept us going, and most especially, the founders of The Chiles Academy: Ms. Anne Ferguson, Ms. Tammy Jones and Ms. Janet Bordenave, who created and have sustained their vision of this school for 14 years.

The Florida Writers Foundation is a proud sponsor of this book.

Michael A. Pyle, President of Armstrong Media Group, LLC
Facebook/Armstrong Medio Group, LLC

I learned of The Chiles Academy in Daytona Beach, Florida, a charter high school for teen moms, on the Internet. The following day I toured the school. Soon, I was invited to visit a reading class. Some students were trying their hands at writing journals, poetry and short stories. Staff spoke of creating an anthology of their work. I suggested publishing it as a book, which would be available on the Internet, so their words of wisdom could inspire others, beyond friends and family.

I invited Veronica Helen Hart to attend a writing session, and the magic of the school pulled her in too. We've been working with the students for months. When we let them choose the cover and then showed actual pages of their text their eyes lit up.

I thank the students who devoted their time to writing pieces and staff of The Chiles Academy for the opportunity to publish this book. The enthusiasm of the students was all we needed to know this was the thing to do. I also specifically thank Glenda Taylor, Veronica "Ronnie" Hart, the executive staff, including Anne Ferguson, Executive Director, front office staff, specifically including Sheryl Bell who was relentless in trying to obtain documents we needed, the Board of Directors, the teachers, specifically including Nfrwi Hall, for their support. Lastly, we thank the Florida Writers' Foundation, which is related to the Florida Writers' Association, for donating funds to help with the costs of publication and providing copies of books to the students and the school. The great majority of proceeds from this book will go to the authors and The Chiles Academy or Bonner-Chiles Foundation, which has been created for its benefit.

Veronica Helen Hart, Uppity Women Press - "Books about historical, humorous, adventurous, and always strong women."

www.veronicahhart.com
Facebook/Uppity Women Press

When Michael Pyle invited me to meet with the young women of The Chiles Academy, I did not know what to expect. At the first meeting with about seven students it was obvious they were feeling suspicious and tentative about strangers reading their writings, their personal and often intimate thoughts. As we continued to meet and the trust grew between us, the poems and stories took shape.

I thank Michael for the opportunity to take part in this program. He has already named the staff of the academy, who are always cheerful, supportive, and generous to the students.

It was my pleasure and honor to work with each and every one of the young women. I feel blessed to know them.

Acknowledgment:

The Chiles Academy and the publishers thank The Florida Writers Foundation for their generous grant to make the printing of this book possible. The FWF promotes literacy by enhancing writing skills in children and adults. They partner with existing programs and initiatives as well as developing new programs.

This book is dedicated to Ms. Hope Conroy, a volunteer college student whose generosity of heart and time inspired our students to discover their voices as writers.

It is also dedicated to all teachers and volunteers who spend their time working with and encouraging students to define their voices through the written word.

Dear Chiles Academy Staff,

I feel so proud to finally be able to write this letter. More than 5 years ago I came to The Chiles Academy, a 15 year old teen mom. Still young and trying to find myself, unwilling to listen, with potential that everyone else could see except for me. Mrs. B, Mrs. Jones & Mrs. Ferguson were like mothers to me, no matter how much I disappointed you, you tried with me and put up with my "tantrums." I strayed away from education too many times and you always had faith in me and welcomed me back. I look back on those years now, amazed at how far I have made it. Everyone at The Chiles Academy played a big role in that. When I left Daytona Beach I didn't know how my life was going to turn out. But I must say I am blessed, to have had teachers like you all, a mother that loves me so much and 2 beautiful healthy children, who, by the way, are amazing. My son is now six years old and has started kindergarten and is reading, writing and adding like you wouldn't believe! Joshua is four and is in Head Start. He has such an amazing imagination, he could probably write a novel. He is also grasping everything his teacher presents to him. I'm so proud of them. So much has changed in my life. I'm an independent mother, I'm working as a certified nursing assistant at a skilled nursing facility I have been working at for two years and I also have my own place that I have been in for two years.

But the best news of all, I now have my High School Diploma, and I will be attending Manatee Community College in spring 2009. Associate in Science Degree, here I come!!! I'm going to school to be a registered nurse. I'm kind of nervous, but there are

1

challenges every day in life, I just know that conquering this challenge will drastically change my life as well as my children's for the better. It feels so good for people to come tell me how proud they are, but I am also proud of myself. I feel so confident now and so many more doors are open to me that weren't before. I just want everyone to know how much I appreciate everything they have ever done for me. Mission Accomplished!

Sincerely Yours,

Domonique Black

A New Love

Nola Brown

Looking back to the years before,

Thinking of who I used to be.

I never expected to be here,

Not here, this I never did see.

My life as a child wasn't all that great,

So you wouldn't expect to see me here.

Life back then was so full of hate,

My future was never clear.

Growing up without my dad,

Was the best, at first.

Not knowing that one day,

It would cause a world full of hurt.

Thirteen years later,

He was sitting in front of me.

To me he didn't exist,

So I asked myself, who could this be?

He took me here, he took me there,

He took me to places I had never seen.

In just one day he became my best friend,

It never crossed me that he would be so

green.

We sat at the creek,

When it was time to leave I came to see,

In that one day he opened my eyes

To a whole new world of nature and

beauty.

I woke up the next morning,

As happy as I could be.

Not knowing that the man I met,

Never again would I see.

That's when it started,

I would never love anyone that way
again.
Down through the years all I could do
was hate,
I didn't want to have friends.
He was supposed to be my hero,
Not the villain who broke my heart.
I was just a child, but I fell for it,
The plan he had from the start.
I was so young that I couldn't
understand,
Or maybe I didn't want to.
I wasn't really sure why,
I didn't know what to say or what to do.
Growing up I should've known,
That one day he would be back.
Every day that wall became bigger and
bigger,
My heart just couldn't allow that.

Years later I found out I was pregnant,
And I almost fell apart.
All these years I never learned how to
love,
And now I didn't know where to start.

Within a few months I had this strange
feeling,
That I had never felt before.
It was a very warm, and tingly feeling,
One I couldn't possibly ignore.
There was something special growing
inside of me,
And I wanted the whole world to know.
I couldn't wait for him to get here,
Everyday my love for him would grow.
Thinking of my childhood,
And the hate that was there.
I couldn't leave my child alone,

Just a second without him I couldn't
bear.
So now when I think about my life,
My son is the only thing I see.
I've completely changed into a new
woman,
I'm not the girl I used to be.

Mind...
Mary Butler

"How many times am I going to have to tell you no, Jessica?" My mom's voice was firm, however I could sense that her resolve was weakening.

For the past week, I'd been begging my mom to let me wear a dress to school. I wasn't really the frilly type, and had no real desire to wear a dress. You can't dig for earth worms in a dress, you can't play on the jungle gym in a dress, and worst of all, you can't swing in a dress. No, I was out to prove myself to the most arrogant girl I had had the misfortune to meet in all five years of my life. She pranced around in all of her glory, like she *owned* the place, which she might as well have considering that her mother was the teacher for our age group.

For the most part, I tried to steer clear of Samantha. There were a few girls that practically threw themselves at her in order to enjoy certain luxuries like being favored over other children and receiving special treatment, which they couldn't afford without being "friends" with Samantha.

I, on the other hand, didn't need Samantha's friendship or even approval to obtain these things and it undoubtedly rubbed her the wrong way. Our paths rarely crossed, and the few times they did, I was as courteous as possible.

Not because I was intimidated by her status, or even by her mother. I was as nice as I knew how to be because I didn't know very much about this girl. I only knew the things that I saw for how I saw them, and also because she'd never actually done anything to me. So maybe that's why when I saw her standing there, alone on the playground that day, I complimented her on her dress.

"That's a really pretty dress, Samantha. I have one just like it." I hadn't lied either. The rosy red, knee length, spaghetti-strapped dress with Tweetie bird printed in the pocket suited her thin frame and wispy dirty blonde hair. I did have the exact same dress hanging in the back of my closet at home.

"I don't believe you." Her reply was icy; she didn't even look in my direction. She just continued twirling her long hair and chewing haughtily on her gum, which wasn't even allowed in school…unless your name was Samantha and your mother was the teacher.

"Yes I do!" I shouted, my hands balled into tiny fists of fury on each side of my small body.

"Not only do I not believe that you have this dress, but I don't believe that you've got one single dress at all. You wear pants, not even pretty ones, every single day." Samantha still wasn't looking at me, which only made me that much more angry. "I've got tons of dresses that are even prettier than the one you're wearing. I have the prettiest dress of them all." Only then did Samantha slowly turn and look my way, wearing the snidest smirk of all snide smirks.

"Prove it." She said no more and didn't allow me the opportunity to respond as she walked across the platform we were standing on, and slid neatly down the slide.

I'd show her.

I spent the rest the rest of the day in a big huff, plotting how I would exact my revenge on Samantha. I could see myself now, strutting in the door tomorrow morning, sporting my crisp, white, ruffled dress.

Samantha's outfit would pale in comparison and as all the other girls flocked in my direction, Samantha would be forced to sit alone and wallow in the feeling of being upstaged. My plan would've gone without a hitch, had I not forgotten one major detail…

"Absolutely not, Jessica. You may not wear a dress to school. I've seen the way you are out there on that playground. You won't be crawling and climbing all over the jungle gym for little boys to look up and see your panties."

"But Mom—" My sentence was cut short by the sound of my clothes for the day hitting the mattress with a quiet thud.

My mom walked out the room, meaning she was through with that conversation, and called from the hallway, "You can pick your shoes, though." I went to school that day and offered the flat excuse that my dress was being washed so that tomorrow it would be extra white and pretty because girls don't wear dingy clothes. The next day, I laid the dress across the bed before my mom came in to pick out my clothes. She didn't say much but good morning because we were running late for school, and when she turned from the dresser to the bed only to find the dress, her annoyance with me was clear.

Before she could say anything, I launched into pleading. "Please, Mom, please? I promise I'll be good. I won't go on the playground after lunch, or even after story time. I'll sit in chairs not the floor all day with my legs crossed, just like this." I then proceeded to model just how prim and proper I would be by seating myself daintily on the bed, crossing my legs, and keeping my back straight as a ruler. I even flashed what I thought to be a modest smile in my mom's direction. She glanced exasperatedly at her watch then turned back toward the dresser and began fingering through the clothes. My heart sank along with my perfect posture.

"This is it," I thought to myself. I would have to deal with Samantha's silent ridicule for the rest of my days; maybe even until elementary school. My mom tossed a pair of shorts onto the bed and I couldn't even stand to look at them. "What about a shirt?" I asked resentfully.

"No shirt, I'm going to let you wear the dress."

"Really?" I sprung to life in an instant, and reached for the dress.

"That's on two conditions. One, you're wearing shorts under it. Two, if you get anything on this dress, and I mean anything, I'm gonna' light you up like a Christmas tree as soon as you get home."

I nodded feverishly, slipped on the dress and then a pair of white sandals. I could only think of one other thing that could make it look better and that would be the look on Samantha's face when she saw it. The entire car ride to school, I was so excited that I could barely sit still. I fidgeted something terrible while Mom conversed with Miss Anna in the front office and when the time came for me to walk into the play room, it was exactly how I imagined it would be. All conversation ceased when I entered the room as the other children gazed in admiration of my beauty. I guess that Samantha must have thought that her mother or one of the other teachers had called for quiet time, because she continued chattering on. But when her cronies failed to respond, she looked up and saw me.

"Can I touch it?" said Julie. I smiled warmly at her.

"I'm sorry, Julie, but it is very important that I keep this dress clean." She seemed a bit disappointed at first, but she nodded her head knowingly and complimented me one last time before going back to what she was doing.

So went the rest of the morning. I held true to my word and sat in chairs, rather than on the floor. Even during nap time, I didn't take one in order to avoid being on the floor. I stayed up with Samantha and her mother while all the other children slept. I didn't particularly care for Samantha's mother because she showed such obvious favoritism towards her daughter, but she and I had a very riveting discussion about this week's lunch. We complained about the canned green beans and praised the white grape juicy juice flavor they'd recently started serving. Everything was going grand until she announced that we would be having spaghetti today for lunch.

I was mortified sitting at the lunch table. I considered skipping the meal altogether, but Ms. Anna insisted I eat. When the tray of spaghetti and corn was placed in front of me, I opted to start with the corn. Samantha was acting different than she had for most of the day. She seemed more cheerful, which led me to believe that something was up. I couldn't worry about whatever it was now, though. I had to focus all of my energy toward getting every forkful of the spaghetti safely into my mouth. Ten minutes and about twenty scoops later, I had one more scoop to go. I was tearfully joyous as I brought the last scoop to my mouth, and that's when it happened. I shouldn't say happened; it's more like what *Samantha* did.

I felt it first; a slimy damp sensation. I dropped my fork and dared to look down to find that the entire front of my dress was covered in spaghetti, and to my right, there was Samantha laughing harder than the hyenas from The Lion King. I did what any kid would do; picked up the first thing my hand touched, and chucked it at her as hard as I possibly could. Unfortunately for both of us, that thing happened to be a fork. Samantha's scream rang through the small dining area, as blood poured from each of the fork's four prong holes. All of the children were escorted out of the room, except for me. I had the pleasure of watching an EMT pull the fork out of Samantha's forehead.

I thought that getting back at Samantha would make me feel better, but it only made things worse. When my mom arrived at the daycare, she lit-me-up like not just *any* Christmas tree; but like the Christmas tree in Times Square. Samantha and I never spoke again. In fact, I don't remember even seeing her again after that. What I will always remember about this incident, however, is that white is *not* my color.

Sperm Donor

Rodaisha Matthews

Baby daddy, baby daddy, where do I begin?
You're a little boy for disclaiming your kid
Your son is a blessing and you're too dumb to see it
You're a disgrace to mankind
You make me sick to the point I can't help but forgive you
You're a dog who needs to be trained
How can you keep bringing kids in this world and not
providing for them?
You swear you're a real man but real men take care of
their seeds
I know you're going to need my son before he needs you
All I want you to be is a daddy instead of a sperm donor
Your son can be a hero and save your life
Why would you not want to wake up in the morning and
smother him with smooches?
He likes to pounce on his tiger and play in his litter of toys
His smile just lights up a whole room
Your son is an amazing kid he is so smart for his age
He loves to walk and hold on to things
He can't stay still; he's just a busy baby
Every day he brings so much joy in my life
I love our son
I would die for him
When he grows up I'm going to teach him how to treat a
woman right, unlike how you done me.

When My Life Changed
by MLH

My life changed dramatically when I found out I was pregnant. I felt horrible and scared. My mom and dad were very mad at me because they expected the best from me and wanted me to succeed in life. I was kicked out of public school for the rest of my seventh grade year. I didn't go to school for about a month. The school told me and my mother that I could do my work at home and turn it back in, but I never received any work that I needed to complete. My mom went to the school like every other day to see if any work of mine was collected and sent to the office for her to pick up, but there never was, so for a month I did nothing school related, but still they passed me on to the next grade.

After the summer was over and school was about to start up again, my mom had done some research in finding me a school to go to and that's how she found out about The Chiles Academy. When I discovered I was pregnant I was like six months along. I didn't have any symptoms of being pregnant, so I just didn't know. When school started my son was only a few weeks old.

This school helped me in so many ways like free childcare for my son, a great support system, being able to get clothes for my son and, most important, getting an education and graduating high school. This school has helped me out a lot with my grades when before I was barely passing. At The

Chiles Academy I have received a lot of help when I needed it and now I'm making honor roll.

In middle school I didn't really get along with students and sometimes not even the teachers, I was always getting into fights over stupid things. And getting suspended. And missing out on school. At The Chiles Academy I get along with everyone and there isn't anyone trying to cause problems. And that's definitely because everyone is older and way more mature here. We all have kids or are expecting to have a kid.

I appreciate the help I get from this school and I love coming here with my son. My life changed so much being a teen mom, but I wouldn't change anything because I love him. I am very grateful for this school.

My Hero
by Ashley Hands

A hero is an extraordinary person who will appear in your life at some point or has been there the whole time and isn't noticed for a while. Heroes contain special qualities that most normal people do not possess. Some of those qualities are bravery, honesty, leadership, and selflessness. A lot of heroes are brought up or raised in a unique environment. I have a hero in my life. His name is Andrew and he is my uncle.

My Uncle Andrew is my hero because he has been there for me my whole life, but I didn't realize that until my dad passed. At that point in my life my mom wasn't giving me the support I needed, neither were my grandparents. Even though he was the one who had more to deal with because he was the one who found my dad, Uncle Andrew gave me the courage to move on. He is now the closest person I have to my dad.

Every day he does amazing things. No matter how much is on his mind he is always calm and collected. He deals with customers daily that I would never have the patience to deal with. He deals with everyday pressure so well. Andrew is very strong emotionally and physically. He is also a constant reminder to me of how hard work will bring success and that no matter what is thrown at me I can handle it. He has also convinced me that the right person for me and my daughter will come around. I just need to be patient.

Over the years my uncle has also guided me through hard times and physically affected my life in heroic ways. One way is he helped my grandparents with paperwork and phone calls to save my brother and me from my mother and foster care. While I was in foster care he explained why I should make the decision to come to Florida so I wouldn't risk losing my daughter. He also helped me make another important decision, and that was whether or not to leave the father of my child. I was so blinded by my love for him that even after I found out he cheated on me I couldn't see that he didn't care about me or his daughter. That is one thing that to this day I cannot thank Uncle Andrew enough for.

Those are the reasons my uncle is my hero. I love him so much and I wish there was more I could do to thank him for being in my life. He is one of the strongest people I know. Andrew works so hard and deserves all the good things that have or will happen to him. I hope he is in my life for many years to come so that my little girl can see and understand why I look up to him and see him as my hero.

Dedicated to my Hero, Andrew Hands

You and I

Sharonda Daniels

You are the petal on the flower

You are the leaves on the branch

You are the stars in the sky

You are the moonlight lighting up the
ocean

You are the wheels on the bus

You are the Boo in Peek

You are the key to my heart

You are the dimples in my smile

You are the groom in my wedding

You are the flames in the fire

You are the wings on the birds

The crown of the king.

You are the bullet in the chamber

You are the soldier in the battlefield.

You are the father to our sons

Me, I am the leap in the ballerina

I am the berry in your fruit

I am the sun that brightens your day
I am the smile in your frown
I am the dream in your sleep
I am the lock on your heart.
I am yours, like you are mine.

I Like You
Kayvon Brown

You are the light to my moon

The twinkle in my eyes.

You are my favorite foods on a tray,

And the juice that fills my cup.

You are the blue in the sky,

And the green on the grass.

It might surprise you that,

I am the beat in a heart,

And a beauty without a beast.

I also happen to be the take away of your
breath,

The rose that blooms
without the sun.

Dear Janewella, a letter to herself

Dear Janewella,

I would like to start off by saying love yourself first. Be happy, be vigilant and always put God first. Life is like a roller coaster - what goes up comes down. In life there will be times when you're feeling unwanted and helpless. There will be things that are beyond your control. But don't give up.

Getting pregnant at such a young age, and being forced to live with a stranger having to abide by their rules and putting up with it. Just stay humble even at your boiling point. Prove those that said you weren't going to make it wrong. Achieve your goals and don't let anybody tell you otherwise. The sky is not the limit. Make plans, set goals and achieve them. Go for what you believe in. Yes, you may feel like giving up, you may feel like everything is not going as planned but don't give up. Be humble and have patience. Everything doesn't happen overnight.

Take every opportunity and advantage that life throws at you. As you get older you'll eventually see what life is really about.

Be aware of "friends". Everyone is not your friend some people just don't want to see you come up.

Be careful of the people you chose to vent to, "a listening ear is also a running mouth".

Never settle for less because you deserve the best.

You can take on the world if you put in work and make your parents proud. When you fail get back up and try again. You won't always make it on your first try but be persistent and aggressive.

Always speak your mind.

Please listen to your parents they know what is best. Don't think of it as that they're trying to ruin your life. It's for the best for you and later in life you'll look back at that moment and be grateful that you listened. Take heed and choose wisely.

It's okay to be different; don't feel like giving up. Everyone else is not going to see your vision, because it's not everyone else's journey. Always have the mentality that you're going to make it no matter what. Don't settle for less.

Respect your body and yourself; you are intelligent, you are beautiful, you are unique, you are a child of God.

You are Janewella James.

Repugnant
Moon Child

You are the mis in mistake,
The no in oh-no,
The sick feeling in the pit of my stomach,
The gum on the bottom of my shoe.

What you will never be is the
reason
For my smile, the reason why I
work hard.
Your absence is defining who you
are.
How can you call yourself a man
When you have no man abilities or
thoughts?

You are the one negative thought
That destroys all the positive ones,
The thought of us being something at one
point, makes me feel so indisposed.
Your presence is not like the smell
of butter pecan pie on a Sunday
morning or the soothing sound of
a harp...

But I am the feeling of triumph
after a war fought for victory,

I am the light in the dark room,
The reincarnated soul of a lion,
The beauty of Aphrodite,
The swiftness and intelligence of Harriet
Tubman

I am phenomenal.

HARRIET TUBMAN.

My Son
by Darby Beaudry

You are the sparkle in my eye,

The sunshine I wake up to,

The soul that makes me complete,

You are not the burden people thought
at first,

Nor a mistake.

You are the oxygen to my brain,

The blood that fills my heart-break,

I am the person you look up to,

I am sweet like cake.

I am your mommy.

Personal Narrative

Katt Powell

I always told myself my purpose in this world was to become a mother. Even as a child growing up without a mother, I still managed to become the parent I am today. Baby dolls after baby dolls and lots of observing of younger children and their mothers is where I got my strength to do what I do today for my child. After nine months of preparing for the day, he was in my arms. It was the day I changed, my thoughts changed, my life changed, my perspectives and everything else around me changed.

All it took was a trip to the store and a pee on a stick to change my life. I was shocked but I couldn't help feel happy about expecting. I always knew I'd make a great mom but at eighteen but I was often questioned and went through mixed emotions, along with hormones raging. I always ended up with the same thought, I can do this, I have no choice but to do this.

My goal to becoming a mother and being a mother was "No matter what."

Most said "a baby having a baby" but is there really any right time or age to have a kid? Considering I had my mind made up to do this, I let comments go in one ear and out the other. I had my own home and was with the father (somewhat) which made me feel better. It takes a certain person to do what a mother does.

~*~

November twenty-eighth is when my life really changed. I thought just knowing I had a little growing spirit inside me was the change. It started with one intense pain

27

in the middle of eating my bar-b-que pulled pork sandwich at Dustins. I knew that day it was almost time. That night I spent five hours in the steaming shower holding on to the wall, as if I was going to go somewhere after every contraction, forcing myself to jump or walk around the house to force this baby more into the birth canal. My labor was on Thanksgiving. After getting sent home for not being far enough dilated, there was no way I was going to miss out on all the dank Thanksgiving food. It would be my last time for a while to eat with both my hands and without getting interrupted by my little one. I went on with my day with contractions every two to five minutes, slowly eating the warm sweet potato casserole with melted marshmallows and sugar pecans on top, which I craved my whole pregnancy. I could taste it and the turkey before it even hit the fork. I managed to savor every last bite of that Thanksgiving meal, even if it'd make me regret it with my head in the trash can. My plan was to rest but it seemed the moment I finished my filling meal it made the baby move where he wanted to go. The contractions grew closer and longer and more painful. I remember crying to my mother like a baby. Yes, this was my only time during my whole labor I tolerated someone saying "a baby having a baby". I just wanted my mother to hold me again.

Back to the hospital we go. I get in my gown and after all the tests, it was for sure I wasn't going home. I would be having my baby. It hit me all over again, just fifty times harder, almost like a train hitting me or going through me. They hooked all these wires up to me and gave me a big thick needle right in the middle of my spine. Then all a sudden, it worked like magic and all my pain went away. Well it didn't exactly go anywhere but I could no longer feel it. Might as well call it magic. Soon I was able to rest my drooping eyes for a little to make up for the long prior twenty four hours they had been awake. Waking up to "Honey it's time to push" was not exactly what a person normally wakes up to but at that moment, that is ALL I wanted to hear. My legs were numb and I'm not sure if that was from the epidural or from sitting in the same spot in bed for hours. So we began the huffing and the puffing and the *oh no's* and the constant counting, "One-two-three, one-two-three," feeling like my eyes were going to pop out before this baby would. All of a sudden there were baby cries, MY BABY cries. I never cherished his screaming as much as I did that day. Brave was here. All my pain and tiredness and stress flew out the window, vanishing.

The world then paused around me. All I saw, thought, breathed, and heard was my son. The feeling a mother gets through her body when holding her baby for the first time is almost unexplainable. It's like you just stop and pause and suddenly nothing matters to you expect that baby. At eleven p.m., when he took his first breath was when my life changed; when the realness settled into my mind. I was this innocent child's mother, protector, teacher, and nurse and so much more. It was insane to the point my face hurt from smiling, knowing that I was all that to him. Staring at him with his pink skin so soft, I found myself constantly running my fingers lightly on his sleeping face and over his still fetal positioned body, like I still do to this day.

Isaac, My Love

Ivette R.

You're the air that I breathe,

My strength through it all.

Nothing can compare to the day I held
your fragile body for the first time.

My best friend, my everything,

I couldn't be more proud of you.

Though I may not be able to give you
riches and the latest trends in toys.

The Lord truly blessed me with my little
piece of joy. I love you, yes, I do.

Isaac, I am blessed to call you my son,
and proud to be your mommy. I love
you.

Not Too Good of a Dad

Sarah Winters

You could have been the sunshine in
my life,
But instead you are the dark alley I
would never travel down twice.
You are the P in pain that runs
through my heart every time I hear
your name.

You used to be the smile across my face,
But now you're the sick feeling in my
gut.
Those late nights sitting up with you
watching TV, cuddling,
Used to make my heart warm up like a
350 oven.
But now I wish I could throw the
memories out the window.

But now I am the sun and moon,
And everything important to living.
I am the food God gave me to eat.
I am the water that I need to drink,
but not only am I all that,
I am everything better than you will
ever be.

My Personal Manifesto

Morgan Beach

I am definitely a Pisces

I'm compassionate, kind, selfless, sensitive, easygoing, understanding, observant, and intuitive. I'm an escapist, secretive, emotional, easily misled, and idealistic. My most creative skills are shown in music and literature.

When it comes to my friends and family, I have more concern for their problems rather than my own. I'll agree that it's a good thing to be kind, but sometimes people take my kindness for granted. Because I'm so selfless, I always have a habit of putting other people before me. I need to learn to love myself because I may be put into a situation that I wouldn't want to be in. I'm easygoing and understanding, I feel that I can use these abilities to be a reliable friend. I'm observant of body language and intuitive when it comes to those around me, especially the ones I love. In other words, I know when something isn't right. I can sense when a person is lying, and sometimes I can feel a person's needs.

I'm an escapist when it comes to arguments or situations that I don't want to be in. I need to learn to stand my ground more and fight for me. I've realized that I've become too emotional, which causes me to be secretive at times because I don't want to bring someone else down. Sometimes I'm easily misled, which causes people to take control of me and my life. It's time to start doing what is right, even when it's really hard. I need to stop letting people walk over me.

I believe in natural beauty.

People tell me that I am beautiful. I don't wear make-up because I believe that it hides my true identity. I believe that no matter what you change about yourself, you'll still have the same beauty that makes you you.

In my opinion, natural beauty is when you are yourself by nature; you do what you feel is right, you stand your ground, and you always show your true personality without thinking about it.

I feel like make-up is a waste of time and a waste of money.

What I want most in the world is to be independent and successful.

I am dedicated to making a better life for me and my son. I want to show the world that even though I'm young, I can still accomplish the same independence as an adult.

I'm tired of having to depend on other people for things such as money, clothes, shoes, and even food. I want to have my own things and I want to get these things on my own. The constant worry about if someone is going to get what I need for myself or my son is too much. I feel that as a mother I need to be the one to carry on the responsibility of getting these things and I feel a little ashamed of myself because I don't have any way to get the finances I need to be independent. To accomplish my independence and success, the first thing I need to do is get a job. Then I need to open a banking account and deposit about $50 into it every paycheck to save for a car and emergencies. When I turn eighteen, I need to create my own case so that I can apply for food stamps and get my own place to stay under the housing authority. I will continue to work hard on my high school ethics to show that I can be independent. Once I get all of these things situated, I will go to college to be a cosmetologist.

I believe the most important thing in a person is to be honest.

Honesty is what keeps all relationships together; it's what defines who a person is. Honesty is what you need to know the truth, even if it's the kind you want to avoid.

If you can be honest with yourself, you can be honest with everyone else as well. I feel that being honest is the hardest thing for anyone to do. Why? Because on negative terms, you want to avoid the arguing, you want to ease yourself out of difficult situations; you want to avoid hurting yourself in the process and causing emotional pain toward someone else. Yet, on the positive side, you'll know what you've been yearning to find out. You can move on from a situation, keep yourself out of trouble, and you can love yourself more, as well as someone else.

I need to continue to be honest with my feelings, with some of my problems and a few of my differences. Even if nobody wants to hear my truth, I need to be honest no matter how a person feels because it means that I am being honest with myself; it means I'm standing my ground for my rights and my dignity. Sometimes being honest is what a person needs to do to break down that "wall of mistrust."

I will stop going to everyone about my problems.

The world doesn't need to know everything about what I'm going through. Saying too much can cause a person to get in the middle of a situation or may lead to trouble. *Everyone* will be in my business.

I need to stop talking to outsider about my problems. One reason is because people will see me as someone who is emotionally dependent all of the time; someone who is too much drama; or as someone who is always complaining about something. Another reason is because I don't want to feel like a burden toward everyone. In other words, I don't want them to get irritated with me if I'm always going to them about something wrong. I say this because I know they have to be tired of hearing about it and they might feel like they have things of their own to worry about. Also, I don't want to be the "talk of the town." If I'm to tell one person about something, you might as well say that the whole world knows every detail about it, or worse, they may hear something different from what was actually said, and then the rumors begin.

To solve the issue, I need to stop telling outsiders about certain situations that go on inside of me and my life. Sometimes the best thing is to know when to handle something on your own, and how to recognize when you need help from a trusted counselor.

I need to show everyone that I can be independent in my thoughts, my needs, and my issues; that I can take care of myself at times. I need to talk to the person individually who had offended me in some way, and be mature about the situation by talking everything out in a calm manner instead of lashing out.

You Don't Know Me

Octavia Laboo

You haven't seen the tears I cried or the
pain I hide.

All you see is this big brilliant smile

But you haven't felt the pain I felt, and
all the days I wept.

You haven't seen the horrible things that
happened to me.

You think you know me.

That's a lie, because you don't know me.
Not even one bit.

You haven't heard the lies my ears heard.

But you say you know me.

You haven't had all the put downs and the "*you can'ts*" or "*you never wills*" I have endured.

But yet you still say you know me.

All you know is the big brilliant smile and a laugh that says everything is fine

But look at me, look at me close.

See past the smiles and the laughs, look in my eyes and tell me you see what I see.

When you see the lies, heart aches, broken promises and the tears,

Then you can say you know, but for now, you don't know me.

Jasmine Dilliard

Dear My Thirteen Year-old Self,

Listen, I am warning you now the way you're acting is just going to lead you to a life of mischief and heartbreaks. You need to stop a lot of the things you are doing. For example, that boy Xavier you're talking to. Yeah, he is just going to get you in trouble, he is going to get you caught up in a life you don't want, he is going to get you hurt not only physically, but mentally. You will be damaged. Another example: You know the twins Brittany and Hayley? They will set you up to fight a girl that was more your friend then they were. I am just going to stop here and explain in detail how your life is going to end up by sixteen.

By the time you're fourteen, you're still talking to that boy who lives in Iowa. You're in love with him. You find yourself getting in an argument with your parents and end up running away after school. You started to walk on that highway that night by the Roadway Inn where you're staying at the time with your parents. Then a green car pulls over and there's an old man in the car. He asks if you need a ride. You say yes, thinking nothing is going to happen to you. He is an old man, what can really happen?

I am thinking to myself. Well, guess what, a lot happens.

He starts off by drugging you up. He takes you to his house and he takes advantage of you, then sends you to some of his friends and they keep you hostage. They drug you, they rape you, and they threaten you with their guns. They put the gun to your head they damage you for life. You don't know what to do. You wish you would die. It will be only a week because the cops find you, but the week will feel like years and then you go home.

The nightmare don't end there. You got two more years of nightmares you have to go through.

There appears to be an acceleration in the growth of disappointing news in your life. You're fifteen now and you and your family move to Daytona Beach, Florida to get away from Pennsylvania and now you're talking to this Spanish boy. He is a really shy boy and he barely talks to you while you two date, which is only a month because Izaiah lied and said you liked another boy. When he broke up with you, you were very angry. There was a boy who was cool with so you think about how you can get your ex mad. So you and your dumb ideas said let me hook up with his friend. Yeah, your ex didn't care so let's not even talk to his friend cause it not going to end well at all.

You are going to meet this boy that your sister is dating and he's going to tell you not to talk to him. I am going to need you to listen to him and listen well. These are his friends and he's telling you not to fall for any of those boys because he is right.

You are also going to meet a girl your cousin is going to hook up with, but after he stops talking to her you need to stop talking to her too cause she's going to talk about you when you aren't around.

Also that year you're going to meet a boy that you will have to deal with for the rest of your life and oh my god you are going to hate him, he is going to give you a life of trouble, trust me, and if you don't believe me let me tell you what is going to happen to you when you turn sixteen.

You're sixteen now and you're going to be visiting Nana in Pennsylvania and your sister is going to take you to the hospital because you're getting random bruises on your legs. Do want to hear some good news? There's nothing wrong with your legs.

Now, do you want to hear bad news? Of course not, but I am going to tell you anyway. You're going to be a mommy with an eight pound baby boy. Oh, and guess what, remember how I said you're going to deal with that boy all your life? Yeah, that's the father. You're probably telling yourself, "I hate him," but you had a baby by him.

Let me say things happen. Everyone was asking the same question, yet Aaden and I never told.

When you gave birth to that eight pound baby boy you would fell in love, real love.

Now you have to deal with your baby's father, but to your surprise he steps up. When you were pregnant he was telling people that wasn't his kid, but when Aaden came he realized it was and he was actually going to be there.

Now tell me, do you want to lose you virginity when you're fourteen to some guy you don't know and don't love? You really want people to talk about you? Do you really want a child at a young age no matter how much you love him don't you want your child be in a nice house with you and your husband being successful so you can give your child everything without struggling? Do you really want this life?

The Things You Missed

Octavia Laboo

You are the scum between my
toes, the grass that hasn't
been cut after a rainstorm

You are the desert heat, the
dry lifeless sand

You are the dried up tears that used to
run down my cheeks

You are not the man you pretended to be

You are not the guy of my dreams

You are not the butterflies in my stomach

You are not the smile on my face

And you are most definitely not the father
you said you would be.

But me, I am strong

I am a lion

I am a queen, a delicate rose swaying in
the cool spring breeze

I am amazing

I am beautiful

I am a soul of a warrior

I am a mother who loves and cares

But most of all I am a father, that you
will never be.

Forever and Always

Veronica Morris

Prologue

∞

"It hurts." His faint voice filled my senses through the phone. "Everything hurts, Kelsey."

I bit down on my lip, worried that he was going to do something drastic. "Are you home?"

He scoffed, "Does it matter if I am?" I could hear the sound of waves. He's at the beach behind our houses. "I can't do this anymore, Kelsey."

"Listen," I told him, quietly sneaking out of my house, not wanting to disturb my parent's slumber. "Wyatt, I know it's hard. I know it is. But you can't give up on yourself. I didn't, and you shouldn't either." I successfully made it onto the ground and began to run toward the beach.

"Kelsey, you know you're my best friend, right?"

"I know, Wyatt. You're my best friend too."

"I love you...I love you more than you'd ever know. I've always loved you, forever and always, sweetheart."

Finally, I made it to the beach. It was small, so it'd be easy to spot him. "I-I love you, too, Wy. Forever and always." I whispered the last part, though I'm sure that he heard it clearly through the phone.

There was only silence on the other end.

"And, Kel?" he finally said.

I sighed, grateful to hear his voice once more. "Yes?"

It went silent again.

"I'm not at the beach." He paused and continued, saying six more words, six more words that will haunt me. "I love you, forever and always."

After that the phone went silent.

"Wyatt? Wyatt!?" I called, but I heard nothing besides the constant sound of waves crashing against something large. I felt sick to my stomach, waiting for some sort of response to let me know that everything was all right but nothing ever happened like that.

Tears burned my eyes as I stood there in silence, the words echoing in my head.

I love you, forever and always...

Forever and always...

Chapter 1
∞

After he had gone silent, I continued to try and find him, hoping to save him.

I frantically dialed the number for the tenth time within five minutes. Still no answer. I continued to search around the shore, when I was pulled in a different direction.

'Sorrow last through the night..."

It was his ringtone, I could hear it but it was pretty faint.

"Wyatt?" I called out. My heart tugged, wanting to hear a response but still nothing. I redialed the number once more. The ringtone was louder this time.

As I continued to walk, I spotted a flashing light. It was his cell phone. I made my way over to the light, hoping that I would find something more hopeful than what I found. Wyatt was lying in the sand with an empty pill bottle beside him.

Everything about the incident seemed to move so fast by that point.

Without thinking about it, I dialed 9-1-1, and stated the address.

"Miss, please calm down and explain your emergency," the dispatcher said trying to calm me. But between the sadness and the shock I couldn't seem to get the strength to even draw a deep breath.

"If you don't calm down you won't be able to help Wyatt," I thought to myself as I went over to him.

"Miss are you still there?" the dispatcher said.

I shuddered and drew a deep breath and used the last of my strength to tell her the details.

"All right, ma'am, an ambulance is on its way, please stay where you are." This was urgent and all she could tell me, was that the ambulance would be here shortly. God, how I hated that.

I sat on the ground beside Wyatt and lifted his head to place it on my lap. Tears streamed down my cheeks as I looked at him. "Wyatt, if you can hear me, I want you to know that I…I always loved you," I said.

I held him, until I heard the EMT staff exit their vehicle. Only then was I aware of the flashing lights, a group of men and women working on him as they put him on a stretcher. They were all yelling orders to each other, and nothing was processing through my mind.

They asked me a million questions, such as, "Were you involved? What did he take?" The one that woke me up was, "Have you called his parents?" I needed to let them know about their son and fast.

I found his mother's number; thankfully I had the whole family on speed dial just in case something were to happen.

"Hello?" a groggy voice sounded on the other end. She must have been sleeping.

"Mrs. Howell, please you have to get up and start heading towards the hospital," I said as I saw Wyatt's body being lifted into the back of the ambulance. "Wyatt…Wyatt tried to overdose," I said, the words getting stuck in my throat as I said them.

I didn't know if she had heard me completely until I heard her yell to Wyatt's dad, telling him to hurry up and grab the car keys, she sounded hysterical herself, but then she must have realized that I was still on the phone. Sounding like she was holding back from crying anymore, she spoke again.

"We'll be there, you go with him to the hospital," she said and hung up the phone.

I placed the phone in my pocket. "Miss, are you coming?" the medic questioned. Without much thought running through my head I climbed in, my eyes focused on Wyatt's face while my hand reached out for his, squeezing it tightly.

"Why couldn't I have seen this coming?" I thought as the sirens wailed and we took off to the hospital.

To Mom, Dad, Matthew, Jenna, Kelsey and all the rest of my loved ones:

I was never much of a happy person. Whoever was close to me knew this very well. Things just got harder to deal with, and I didn't know how to fix things. As many of you know, I began to seclude myself and even started to self-harm myself. It is not something I advise anyone to give into. The harm just wasn't enough, It helped me cope with the pain on the inside, but it just didn't fully help.

What I attempted may or may not have worked. I am going to write two paragraphs-one if it does work and one if it doesn't.

I love you all very much. Dad and Mom, you raised me better than I deserved. Don't think for one second that this has to do with you because it doesn't. I'm just a bit messed up in the head. Don't worry about me.

Matthew, I wish I could have seen what you turned out to be when you got older, me and you have been through a lot. You better follow your dream and become a chef, buy Mom and Dad a big house so they can live comfortably.

Jenna, you were always a ball of sunshine, know that you are worth so much more than your looks. Please don't give mom a hard time like I did when I was your age.

Now to the love of my life, Kelsey. I love you, beautiful. I loved the time we were together; you made everything so bright for me. It pains me to know that I didn't express my feelings sooner. But I love you, sweetheart. Forever and always. Stay strong for the two of us.

Now what if this attempt was a total bust, well, I'm sorry to put you through the worry and shock. The next time I see you all, I don't want to be flooded with pity. Just know that things like this are going to happen until I figure out how to turn my life around for the best. Like I said, I'm sorry everyone.

Chapter 2

∞

Matt found his note about an hour after Wyatt was admitted into the hospital. Wyatt had it typed up and ready for whoever found it on his dresser marked READ ME in marker. It felt like a dull knife was stuck in my heart with each word in the note.

"Why would he do it?" Robert questioned. His now red, puffy eyes looked at his son, who lay motionless on the bed. Tubes were stuck in his arms and an oxygen mask covered his mouth and nose. His father was told that due to the amount of Xanax he took, Wyatt had initially placed himself in a coma, which how the doctors put 'was not as bad as possibly being dead at the beach' but at this point Wyatt might have been dead.

"They said that Wyatt is in a stable state, but not responding to any of the tests. He could be in a coma for days or even years," Robert said to his wife before his gaze shifted to me. I knew my eyes were red from crying during those hours that we waited to know what was happening with him.

"You were his best friend, Kelsey. Did he say anything to you about any of this?"

I only shook my head in silence. Even though we were best friends we stopped talking to each other toward the end of senior year. I had started dating Jonathan Sykes, and he didn't like how close Wyatt and I were, it aggravated him whenever I told him that I was going to hang out with Wyatt.

"He hasn't said anything about this to me, Mr. Howell," I said.

"It's all right, Kelsey," He said forcing a weak smile and placing a reassuring hand on my shoulder and giving it a gentle squeeze before walking over to his wife, then turned back to face me. "You can go in and speak to him. The doctors said that we would have to leave after that and come back in the morning."

Without thinking twice, I jumped out of my seat and went into the room. I stepped cautiously around the curtain surrounding his bed and sat in the chair already placed close to it. I placed my hand on his, then gently clasped it.

"I'm sorry..." Tears started to run down my face as I tried to think of everything that happened in our lives that could have led up to this. "I'll always be here for you, Wyatt, no matter what..." I said in a whisper as I stood up and leaned over him and gently placed a kiss on his forehead. "I'll be back tomorrow after work," I said, letting go of his hand and leaving the room.

I was expecting to walk home alone, but as I walked out of the hospital someone called out my name.

"Kelsey!" I turned in the direction of the voice and saw Jonathan trotting toward me. He quickly pulled me into a big hug.

"I heard about what happened," he said stroking my hair with his hand as he held me close. "Mrs. Howell told me to come and get you," he said pulling from me a little bit and looking me over. "How are you feeling?"

The question made me want to slap him, how would someone feel knowing that their best friend just tried to kill himself? Was I supposed to feel some sort of joy about that? But I know that he was only being worried about me. "I'm...coping," I said, giving him a fake smile before he started to lead me out of the hospital and toward his car. "I just need to get home and go lie down," I added when I slid into the passenger seat.

"No problem, princess," he said driving me back home.

Chapter 3
∞

After that night, I kept going back to the hospital, either during my lunch breaks or after work. Today was different though. I left work early after receiving a call from Wyatt's mom. She said that there were signs of movement when the doctor was doing tests on him.

Now here I was watching Wyatt. Could I have been dreaming about that call? It all seemed way too good to be true. "I got out of work early; I figured that you would want some company," I said, the same dull pain striking my heart as I spoke those words.

If I kept him company before, this probably wouldn't have happened. My eyes trailed around the room. The monotonous beep of the heart monitor pinged in the background. The whiteboard at the front of the door read Coma Patient in big black dry erase letters and under it Dr. Laverne.

"Please give me a sign or something, Wyatt. Something that will give me hope," I said as I felt the burning sting of tears swell up in the corner of my eyes. "Everyone wants you to come back." I needed him with me, to let me know that everything was going to be all right.

I was so deep in my distressed thoughts that I didn't realize that Matthew and Jenna had walked up behind me until I felt a hand on my shoulder. "My mom told me that he had showed a small sign of coming back to us, nothing too much, but I figured that I would stop by with Jenna. Mom said that you most likely would be here," Matt said with a weak smile.

I knew that he hated coming here, seeing his brother so broken but he was hoping for the same thing as I was...for Wyatt to come back to us.

"Yeah, I just came by," I said trying my best to sound strong, but I knew Matt would hear it in my voice. I was about to say something again when I heard Jenna speak.

"My teacher said that if someone tries to kill themselves they must be weak or they must be trying to hide something."

Those words broke me and I could see the anger in Matthew's face before turning to Jenna, trying to stay calm.

Matt said, "Your teacher is wrong. Wyatt wasn't hiding anything and he was stronger than either of us. When we were kids he proved that every summer despite getting hurt because of it." He continued looking at Jenna, who looked at the tile floor. "There's a reason why we don't ever see our grandparents, Jen," he added.

I knew what he was talking about. Wyatt shared the stories about going to his grandparents for the summer with Matt and coming back home beaten and bruised because of their uncle. Wyatt wanted to protect his brother so he took the most of the beatings and the ones who were supposed to protect him from that just sat around and watched as it happened.

I didn't move here until the end of that summer. Wyatt was seen as an outcast at school, he was a joker usually trying to make people laugh, but I saw past all that. I knew that he was only hiding his feelings. The first time that we ever talked I could have been nicer about it but I at least started a friendship with him.

We were in English talking about Edgar Allen Poe's *The Raven* and he made a joke about it and to this day I couldn't remember what set it off or what he even said, but I stood up and placed my text book on the desk and turned around to face him, his green eyes were wide since I never reacted to him before.

All I said was, "You're not very funny. Your jokes are actually pretty pathetic," and somehow after that he started following me around and trying to talk to me. It took about three months before I started to acknowledge that he was even trying to be my friend. It began slow. First he used the old 'I need help with my homework' and then it moved to sitting together at lunch and then we started talking to each other about anything and everything, from family life to past schools.

But one day, a week before winter break, he came to school in a bad mood. No jokes came from his mouth and he kept his head down. He even ignored me during second period. I wasn't able to get to him until lunch and everything happened so fast, one minute I'm yelling at him for being a jerk and ignoring me and the next minute he's hugging me and telling me everything about his grandparents and uncle, how his brother and him would always get hurt and their grandparents wouldn't help. He had received a letter from his uncle inviting him and the rest of the Howell family to his house. The letter triggered Wyatt's anxiety and he was trying to calm himself. He didn't want me to know about what he had been through but now that I knew, I didn't want him to go anywhere near that place.

We stayed like that for some time. I made sure he was all right and his job was only to feel better. That was the first time I actually saw Wyatt's true side, not that joker half, not the one who wanted to make sure that everyone around him was happy and laughing. Seeing that side of Wyatt made me feel closer to him, but I didn't realize just how wrong I really was until now.

Now I realize that there was so much more to Wyatt that I didn't understand, and I feared that I would never get a chance to understand him if he didn't wake up and come back to me.

Chapter 4

∞

It was apparent that Jenna was shocked by what Matt had said. She never really thought about why they never saw their grandparents. It was understandable though, because Samantha was five months pregnant with Jenna when she found out about the abuse going on with her sons. She didn't want that to happen to her only daughter and so she told her parents that she didn't want any more contact with them until they kicked her brother out for good.

"What are you talking about?" she asked looking at him now. Matt only clenched his fists before running his fingers through his shaggy brown hair; he didn't want to ever have to tell Jenna bout *that* part of the family, but if it meant clearing up everything about Wyatt then so be it.

"Would you like me to leave?" I asked, looking at him as he pulled up a seat and hung his head down. I was expecting to be told to go, but instead he shook his head no and put his hand up.

"I already know he told you, so you can stay," he said before looking up at me with a weak smile on his face before it disappeared as he glanced at Jenna, who was waiting for him to speak again. "Wyatt and I always used to go to Nana's and Papa's house for summer because that was when Mom was the busiest and she needed a babysitter because Dad was working also. But every time we went there Uncle Kevin would go on his alcoholic binge and do drugs before taking out his anger and frustrations on me and Wyatt. It had gotten so bad that Wyatt would try to fight back wanting to protect me but then Kevin would beat on Wyatt a lot more. Our grandparents witnessed a lot of what was going on but never said anything. It took a few years for Mom to catch on. Wyatt was no longer the happy-go-lucky kid. He wanted to stay home and when mom found out she was pregnant with you,

Wyatt knew he needed to stop this." Matthew paused for a moment as he wiped away a few tears that threatened to fall before clearing his throat.

"When summer came, we went to the house like usual but Wyatt had a plan. We had just talked Mom into getting us a cellphone with a camera, it didn't take long after dropping us off for good ol' Uncle Kevin to show up tweaked out and stumbling. Wyatt was sitting in the living room and I was in the dining room pretending to be playing on the phone when Kevin started. First it was a hard slap to the back of the head and then the beatings started, it was my job to record everything that was happening and once it was over, I called Mom. She was only an hour away but I told her that we had forgotten our clothes in the car, she was busy with office work, but she said that would come by during her lunch break. Wyatt didn't like waiting a couple of hours to be able to show Mom but he figured that he could wait it out; we had gotten the proof that we needed. In the end, Mom had seen the video, confronted her parents and brother, and to this day she won't have anything to do with them."

Hearing the story again made my stomach turn into knots as I shifted in my seat. It was an uncomfortable silence before Matthew took in a deep breath and glanced at his brother with a look of admiration.

"Wyatt went through a lot. Dad being a therapist, tried getting through to Wyatt, even got him prescriptions for Xanax to help with the anxiety," Matthew continued now with a soft smile before looking up at me. "It wasn't until the first day that Wyatt met Kelsey that we saw a change for the better. Without even meeting her, everyone knew that she was a light in Wyatt's darkness, which is probably why they were always hanging out during school and after school."

I couldn't help but to blush at those words, I always thought that we just hung out because I called him out on his less funny jokes but somehow I was a light for him. Why did hearing those words make my heart skip a few beats?

Giving a small smile, I looked down at Wyatt and realized that I was holding his hand. It felt right holding his hand, like it was supposed to be there.

"Even now, Kelsey just can't seem to leave Wyatt's side even if she tried," Matthew teased as he noticed her hand. That was when Jenna finally made a sound, chuckling and pointing out how red Kelsey's cheeks were at that moment.

"So why didn't you two ever go out?" Jenna asked.

That was when it got silent once again. I didn't know how to answer that question; it baffled me because I really never thought about dating Wyatt. I always thought of him as my best friend and he seemed to never want to date me or anyone else. Hearing all of this now I started to wonder how everything might've been if we did go out together. Without thinking I looked up at Jenna and smiled. "Nerves I guess. I mean Wyatt on the outside was always talking to people or at least joking around with everyone he met," I explained, chuckling slightly as my phone went off.

Taking out the phone I saw a picture of Jonathan on my screen, not the time I would want to talk to him so I just allowed it to go to voicemail. Putting it back in my bag I looked back up at Jenna and Matthew. "Would you guys like to go out for some Froyo?" I asked them, though it wasn't even a necessary question because they both wanted to grab something to eat. "All right, let's go," I said standing up and taking out my car keys. I was tired but I think hanging out and having fun would be good for Jenna at this point.

Chapter 5
∞

"Bye, you guys, see you later," I said as I dropped Jenna and Matthew off at their house. I was happy that I got to spend time with them, but it seemed like as soon as I drove further and further away from them my heart grew heavier.

Taking in a deep breath I kept driving a few more houses down until I got to mine, my parents' cars weren't in the driveway, but a red jeep was planted firmly in the middle of it with an irritated Jonathan leaning against it. Had he been waiting here the whole time for me to come back?

Putting the car into neutral, I didn't know if I should drive away or confront him about whatever his problem was and why he was in my driveway. I sighed again, placing the car in park and turning off the vehicle.

As soon as I got out of the car and started rummaging through my bag, Jonathan started. "I've been calling you all day, Kelsey. Why haven't you been returning my calls?" he asked, barely able to keep his composure. I've been with him long enough to know when he is nothing more than a ticking time bomb waiting to go off on anything near him. I knew what buttons to push and when to either make him explode or deactivate him.

"I was visiting Wyatt and hanging out with Jenna and Matthew. You do know I have something called a life, right?" I said, annoyed that he would even start this crap right now.

He looked a little taken aback, like he wasn't expecting me to come back so quickly. I thought that that bomb would stop but it seemed to get twice as bad. "Wyatt this, Wyatt that…I'm your boyfriend and you're more worried about some wannabe skater. Think about it Kelsey— he is never coming back." He shouted the last part.

The words made me want to throw up when I heard them. I didn't want to see his face at the moment. Pushing past him, I started to make my way up to my front door when I felt a hand grab my wrist and pull me back.

"We aren't done talking. I told you that I hated seeing you go over there all day every day. Wyatt is basically dead." He said the last part with a smirk on his face. I knew he hated the relationship that Wyatt had with me and I always accommodated my life and friendship for Jonathan, but for him to bluntly say that to me hurt more than anything.

My eyes shifted to look at the ground, I wanted him to leave. "Goodbye, Jonathan," I said, turning away and trying to leave. He gripped my wrist harder and roughly pulled me back. The harsh action caused me to cringe before I turned around and slapped him across the face. "I said goodbye," I said again this time harsher as I glared at him.

His face grew red with anger and his nostrils flared wildly. "You know what, you're going to regret this one day, Kelsey. Just you wait!" he said, storming off to his driver side door, swinging it open and getting in. He cranked up the engine and revved it before backing out and driving down the road making the tires screech as he sped away from my house.

I only stood there in the driveway, not sure what to think or what to do; all I knew was that I was tired.

I walked into my house, dropping my bag onto floor as I made my way into the kitchen. I turned on the light and saw a note on the kitchen counter from my parents saying that they were going out for dinner.

"Perfect," I muttered as my own stomach started to growl. "I guess I'll get some take-out," I said. I pushed my bangs out of my eyes, reached over to a drawer and opened it. I took out a stack of take-out menus, deciding to go with the Chinese restaurant.

"Hello, it's the usual order," I said as the voice on the other end cheerfully said all right and then started yelling the order to the workers in the background. I ordered from them almost every night when Wyatt and I played video games and watched movies. "All right, debit card. Thank you."

Even though the restaurant was only a few blocks away my order would still take thirty minutes to get here so I had time to waste.

Leaning against the counter, I let out a soft sigh thinking about the day's events. Everything seemed so right when I was hanging out with Jen and Matthew, but then Jonathan had to go and ruin it because I wasn't devoting my entire time to him.

The clock read 6:50. "My delivery should be here at 7:20 give or take a few minutes," I said. I placed the menus in the drawer and walked back into the living room and plopped down on the couch, flipping on the television to see what was on, as I thought about everything that had happened from the time I met Wyatt up until now.

"Forever and always Wyatt…I love you," I muttered softly.

Chapter 6

∞

Things seemed to have gone back to normal, somewhat. After the argument Jonathan and I had he decided to leave. I ended up finding out about our split when I saw his announcements on Facebook and Twitter that he was single. I'm not going to lie, I felt hurt that he would dump me without actually telling me. I had to find out about it when he posted up a picture of himself at a party making out with Megan Connor, a cheerleader we went to school with. She had always had her eyes on him, but he never gave her the time of day until now.

I looked at myself in the mirror, my dirty blond hair now had six new purple streaks in it since it was something Jenna wanted to try and do. I needed to get ready for work soon, I had been late twice this week and I could tell that my boss was getting more irritated with me each time.

"Honey, hurry up and get dressed," my father said from downstairs. Sighing I slipped on a pair of black slacks, and a button up white shirt. I could finish getting ready at work. "I'm coming," I said, grabbing my bag and apron before rushing out of my room and down the stairs.

"I'll be back a little late, I wanna go say hi to Wyatt," I announced as I grabbed my car keys from the table and rushed out the door. I hated being a waitress, but it brought in money when I needed it. As I started the engine, I couldn't help feeling like something was different about today, like something good was actually going to happen to me that day.

I turned on the radio, smiling as the song *'Sugar'* by Maroon 5 started playing on the radio, causing me to sing along with it as I continued to drive to the small family diner I worked at. It was a nice little place to be and the people that came in were usually pretty nice. It was the first place Wyatt and I decided to go to when we started hanging outside of school. He had ordered a cheeseburger with a sunny-side up egg and I had called him crazy until he had me try it. I had to admit that it was actually pretty good, just very messy at the same time.

"Why did you have to go and do it Wyatt?" I questioned myself as my heart started to feel heavy with grief as I pulled into the parking lot and parked in my usual spot behind the diner. I could already hear Mr. Stallings yelling, "Order up!" to Mitchell, another waiter. I had been there a year before him. He was sort of quiet and pretty much a pushover. If I needed to do something like wash the dishes I could always talk Mitchell into doing it for me.

"About time you got here," a woman said as I opened my car door and stepped out, then made sure it was locked. "George was wondering if you were going to be in on time today," the owner of the voice said with a light laugh. I looked up to see it was Ms. Stallings. She managed the money and made sure that the place stayed in order, but she was also pretty nice and understanding when it came to me and my life. She knew about school and now Wyatt, so she tried to give me enough leeway to get me through it.

"Yeah, I was on time today, didn't want to make him upset that I was late again," I said with a big smile on my face and putting my hair up in a messy bun and then putting on the black bow-tie. I hated wearing the stupid thing, but they said it looked more professional and I'm not going to argue with someone who pays my bills

"Well, let's go make sure you clock-in on time. That is what's going to really matter in the long run. It's pretty slow right now so it won't be too much for you to handle," the older woman said, turning back around to head back into the building and holding the door for me to walk in.

I did and thanked her, making sure my uniform was in order and looked around the room. The usual customers were there like always, eating their meals or watching TV. The Sunday game was on and some of the older men were grimacing at the TV, a usual Sunday here.

"Look who's on time," Mitchell said, balancing a tray of orders in one hand and walking past me. I only smirked at him and walked over to the computer and punched in my number before tying the apron around my waist and got started for work without much hassle. I had worked this job for a little over a year now and mostly everything came natural to me about this place and the people.

Most were friendly, usually saying thank you and making small talk and then there were people like Mr. Robinson, cold and always acting like the world had it out for him. A small "hello" could make this man the meanest person in the world. He usually sat in the back corner of the diner, drinking a coffee and reading the newspaper. Every so often he would grumble a curse word under his breath before turning the pages loud enough for people to hear him do it. I swore he loved the attention that it got him and deep down he actually liked people and liked having people talk to him but he never knew how to handle it.

I was about to walk over and take his coffee when my phone went off, good thing it was on vibrate or this would have been bad. Ignoring the buzzing in my pocket, I walked over to Mr. Robinson.

"Morning," I said cheerfully. He only looked at me over the newspaper and then looked back at it, a grumble leaving his mouth as I picked up the empty cup. "Can I get you anything else?"

"A coffee...black" he said without looking at me.

I nodded my head and walked back to the kitchen. My phone had started to go off again. This better be an emergency. I ignored the phone once again as I filled up the cup. Once it was filled up, I walked back over to the table and placed it down before rushing into the bathroom, looking at my phone. Five new voicemails and twenty new text messages from Matthew and Jenna.

I quickly called Matthew back; on the second ring he picked up, sounding out of breath. "You need to get down here right now," he said breathing hard.

"Matt, I can't. I'm at work right now, bud" I said as softly as possible.

"But it's about Wyatt…He opened his eyes. He's awake right now. You need to come right now," he said frantically. I could hear the rest of the family in the background cheering that Wyatt had finally woken up.

I didn't know how to feel at that moment, a flood of relief and anxiety clouded my train of thought before I rushed out of the bathroom, not realizing that my phone was still on. "Hey I got to leave right now you guys," I said in a rush as I grabbed my bag from behind the counter.

Mr. Stallings looked at me and then towards his wife. "You can't just leave, you just got here," he said when he noticed his wife wasn't going to say anything.

I didn't have time to protest with him, I needed to leave. "I'm sorry. I'll come in tomorrow," I said looking at him and letting my hair down from its ponytail. He looked at me with anger at this point before turning back to look into the kitchen.

"Don't even bother, I told you when I gave you the job that this wasn't the type of job you can come in and leave whenever you want, just stay gone," he said going back to flipping burgers and then slamming his hand on the bell. "ORDER UP, MITCH!" he yelled out before ripping a ticket off of the rack and starting on the next order.

A part of me wanted to say I was only kidding and that I wasn't going to leave, but the other part of me wanted to be there to see Wyatt. Standing there for a moment, I looked at my phone and saw that it was still on. I looked back at Mr. Stallings who had his back toward me and I then looked at Mrs. Stallings who only looked at me and nodded her head before turning around and cleaning off the counter.

Without a second more, I walked out of the diner and over to my car, unlocking the door and getting in, my heart beating faster as I started it up and pulled out of the driveway and drove in the direction of the hospital.

Chapter 7
∞

Driving into the parking lot of the hospital, I found the closest parking space available near the entrance of the large building.

Something about this made me feel queasy inside as I took my keys out of the ignition and got out of my car and shutting the door before heading up to the sliding glass doors. I could see nurses and doctors running around. Like usual the building smelled like bleach and something that smelled like lemons.

"Hello," a thin blond woman said with a bright smile on her face. "How may I help you?" she finished. Her named tag read Melissa.

I returned the smile, almost ready to tell her, but that was before I saw Matthew in the doorway. "Um, actually I'm fine, I just came to see a friend…His brother is right over there," I said standing on my toes as I pointed towards Matt. The nurse's smile faded a bit before she handed me a clipboard with a list of names on it.

"Sign in," she said pointing to an empty space on the page, as if I hadn't done this a hundred times already. "Keep this on you at all times," she stated bluntly handing a sticker to me and then going back to smiling as she greeted a new group of people walked entering the building.

I made my way over to Matthew, who quickly grabbed my arm and lead me to the room. "Come on," he said wanting me to see Wyatt finally be awake for the first time in months.

We had arrived at the room and all I could see were doctors and nurses crowding around the bed, talking over one another as they looked at each other and then back toward the bed. I was greeted by Wyatt's mom. She was smiling as she pulled me into a big hug and then pulled away as the main doctor walked in.

"Okay, everyone, let's give the young man some space and time with his family," the older doctor said, clearing his throat. He turned to look at Ms. Howell and held up his clipboard, adjusting his glasses slightly before addressing her. "The good news is that his vitals are fine, no real damage from the coma. He may have slight amnesia so bear with him if he doesn't remember his original life so much," Dr. Laverne said flipping over the paper and seeing if there was anything else he needed to go over with the family. "We'll get him into rehab to rebuild his muscles. He's young and strong. I'd say within a couple of weeks. We'll run a few more tests to make sure he is completely all right, but other than that, he'll be good as new in no time," the doctor said as he closed the file and walked out with the student nurses and doctors following behind him.

Ms. Howell turned back to look at me and smiled. "He's been asking about you all morning," she said motioning her head in the direction of the half drawn curtain. I was astonished that he would remember me.

"You know I can hear you, right?" a hoarse voice said from behind it as a silhouette of someone appeared on the bed. It was hard to imagine that it had been several months since I heard that voice.

Ms. Howell only chuckled. "Go on," she said as she motioned for the rest of the Howell clan to follow her out to the waiting room to give Wyatt and me some space for the time. It took me a moment to understand what was actually going on.

"Are you just going to stand there, sweetheart?" his tone sweet, but there was a bit of teasing in it as he chuckled weakly.

Sweetheart? I nearly turned around to see who he was talking to. We'd never been boyfriend-girlfriend. We'd always been friends. But he was just recovering so I set aside my discomfort at the endearment and walked toward the bed and sat on the end of it. I studied him. His blond hair was all over the place and his face was paler than usual from being in the dark room. His eyes met mine. He smiled. "I missed you, sweetheart."

That word again. I tried hard to hold back tears, not wanting to cry in front of him, not now at least. "I missed you too," I said softly, looking up at him, trying to figure out everything that has happened in the past ten minutes of being here, looking at him actually being awake and him claiming me as his sweetheart..

"Can I get a hug or are you that mad at me that you don't even want to touch me?" he said in a hesitant tone. Without worrying about it any longer, I quickly leaned over and hugged him. I buried my face against his chest as I felt tears flow, dropping onto his hospital gown. He had been and still was one of my best friends. Wyatt shushed me, and ran his hand through my hair trying to comfort me the best he could. "Everything is going to be all right," he added breathing in deeply as he continues to comfort me.

I pulled away from him a few moments later and dried my eyes, trying to clean up the running make-up on my face before looking at him again. "How are you feeling?"

He stretched his arms above his head and yawned. "Well, I kinda feel like I got hit by a train and then got run over by a herd of stampeding bulls, so I guess I feel fine," he said in a teasing voice, poking my forehead slightly. "How are you feeling? I heard you came here every day just to see me. Pretty sure Jonathan isn't too happy about that," Wyatt said with a quirky smile.

I bit my bottom lip, not fully expecting him to be aware of me coming over to see him. "Yeah, I just wanted to make sure that you were fine. I figured that you could use some company plus I thought I could use the time to keep

Matthew from wanting to try and draw something stupid on your forehead," I joked back at him this time. "And yeah Jon did get mad, but it doesn't matter now. He and I broke up yesterday. It was bound to happen though, we just never had anything in common really."

"And finally she gets it everybody!"

I scowled at his statement "Ha-ha, very funny," I said rolling my eyes and pushing my bangs off my forehead.

He frowned at what I had said, knowing that he had taken it too far. "Hey, Kelsey I'm sorry I was only playing with you. I guess during my absence your taste for my jokes went away." He gave me a stern look before sighing. "It made me feel good to hear that you came here to visit me every day. I would have thought with me being gone that you would stop seeing me and hang around Jonathan a lot more now," he explained.

How could I remind him that we hadn't been *seeing* one another in that way?

"Jonathan thought I was staying over here too much and it caused a huge argument between us," I said bluntly. "All because I love you." I quickly covered my mouth after the sentence left my lips. It hadn't come out the way I meant. I opened my mouth to explain but he stopped me with his reaction.

His eyes widened as if he were in shock. "You actually mean it?"

I nodded my head before looking down at my lap and pushed my bangs from my face once again. What could I say? "Of course I mean it," I said softly as I glanced up at him with a sigh. I needed to explain that I loved him like I loved my brother or my best friend but the thought soon went away when he pulled me close to him and held me tightly.

"I've been waiting to hear you say that for a few years now, sweetheart," he whispered. I hugged him back and smiled up at him. Our eyes now focused on each other completely. Maybe he was right. Maybe I had been ignoring my true feelings for him. At that moment it seemed like we were the only people in the whole building together as we continued to look each other in the eyes.

Wyatt gave a small smirk before leaning down, his soft lips placed against mine. Everything felt right about this situation now and I didn't want it to end. Kissing him back, I pulled him closer to me before hearing someone clear their throat in the background.

We both pulled apart and looked to see who had interrupted us and saw Matthew. "About time you two finally got together," he said leaning against the doorframe and grinning like a Cheshire cat at us.

"You're a mood killer, ya know." Wyatt lay back down on the bed and groaned, grabbing his head. "My head hurts, I really need to rest," Wyatt said. "Thanks again for coming, Kel"

I knew he was tired, but I still didn't want to see him go back to sleep, afraid maybe he could slip back into the coma. I wanted him to stay up a little bit longer, but I did know that he was still in need of his rest and that he shouldn't overdo it any more than he already had. "No problem." I slid off the bed and leaned over to place a kiss on his forehead, but he quickly leaned up and pushed his lips against might with force before pulling away from me and laying back down against the pillow.

"Are you going to stay here for a little bit?"

I nodded, walking over to the empty chair across from the bed and pulling it over. Wyatt grabbed the remote as if he hadn't been in a coma for months and turned the TV on to *Catfish: The TV Show* on MTV. He looked at me, holding out his hand. I smiled at him and placed my hand in his and watched the show. Someone had fallen for someone over the internet and the other person didn't want them to meet and that was all that seemed to happen in all the shows, but Wyatt and I weren't paying much attention. Instead we talked about everything. I filled him in on all that had happened since that night.

Chapter 8

∞

Wyatt left the hospital three weeks later after some intensive physical rehabilitation, though it took some time for him to adjust to everything.

I had taken a new job at the nearby animal shelter and went to visit Wyatt at the end of my shift nearly every day. Though he was kind of like his old self, he seemed more and more dependent on me. I knew I had to explain to him about my feelings, but the time never seemed quite right. I was grateful that at least one of his parents were home whenever I was there. Then one day he asked me if I'd dress up when I came for my visit on Friday.

When I explained my dilemma to my mother, she told me I had to tell him my true feelings about him.

"But, Mom, he's still so fragile. What if he tries to kill himself again?"

"Is that what he told you about his overdose? That it was because of you?"

"No."

"Then, stop worrying about it. He's a big boy. His parents are getting him counseling. But you can't let him go on thinking you're his girlfriend. It's not fair to him or to you. You have your own college plans."

"I'll tell him tonight."

~*~

I knocked on the door to his house. The sound of dogs barking filled the house as I waited to be let in. "Coming!" I heard him telling the dogs to get out of the way and to behave themselves before finally opening the door for me. His hair was slicked back and pulled into a small ponytail and he was wearing a plain white dress shirt and a pair of black pants. He looked nice but I could tell that he was nervous about something.

He looked at me and cleared his throat. "That dress looks nice on you."

I giggled nervously. We stood looking at each other in silence before he finally realized that it was chilly out.

"Oh, come in." He stepped aside to let me through the front door.

I giggled again, happy to see him with energy like this again.

He wrung his hands, then pushed the front door closed. Before speaking, he licked his lips. "Well, I ordered some Italian. My parents are out with Jenna and Matt so we can hang out for a little bit without being bothered."

He held out his arm, and I linked my arm with his. The aroma of breadsticks and pasta sauce wafted out from the dining room. "It sounds like you had this entire night planned out for us." I said. It was hard to believe such a short time ago he was in the hospital.

The table was set with a white tablecloth, floral patterned dishes, sparkling water glasses and shiny silverware. Steam rose from bowls of pasta and sauce. The bread sticks laid in line on a small platter. A bouquet of vibrant red roses in a vase stood at one end of the table. I was speechless about everything.

"I hope everything is to your liking" Wyatt whispered by my ear.

"Of course, everything is just perfect," I said still looking at the table. My stomach tied up in knots and I thought I might be sick because I knew what I had to tell him.

He removed his arm from mine and placed his hand firmly on the small of my back, leading me closer to the table and pulling out my chair. "I'm glad that you like it, sweetheart," he said as I sat down.

I wondered if I could feel any worse. He didn't even seem to notice. My eyes followed him as he walked over to the opposite side of the table and his seat.

"I'm glad to see that you seem a little better now," I said. Unsure what to do next, I helped myself to some pasta and added sauce. He followed me, doing the same.

Once our plates were filled, and we each picked up a bread stick, Wyatt finally spoke. "Of course I feel better, I get to enjoy this evening with my best friend and now possibly my girlfriend."

"Girlfriend, huh?" I said.

His eyes downcast, he nodded.

"Wyatt," I began as I set my fork down on my plate. "We need to talk."

"That's what I want to do, too. Talk to you forever."

"I mean it. Really talk."

His expression changed to one of worry. "Okay. Want to come down to the basement? I can play you my latest tunes on my guitar while we chat."

He wasn't making it easy for me. "All right. Shouldn't we clear this up first?"

"I'll do it later."

I followed him down to the basement where he used to play music with his friend. New music sheets and drawing lined the walls. A notebook lay open on the table next to the sofa. Wyatt hurried over and put it in the drawer.

"What was that?"

He shrugged. "Nothing."

"Something you don't want me to see."

"Nah. Just some words I was trying to make into lyrics for a new song. It's not very good."

There was something about him that made me think he lied. Before he could react, I rushed over and pulled the drawer open. The notebook was a journal and the last entry was dated the night he'd taken the pills.

No one cares about me or what I will become. I am forever alone and this is the life that I was put into. I want to take control of something. I will take my own life. My family might be disappointed, but I can't take feeling alone anymore. I hate being on medication to control my feelings. Who

69

cares anyway? Not my parents, really. They just want me to be a "good boy" and do well at school. Not my friends. They wouldn't even notice if I disappeared. I need to be free of this cold hollow shell, of the ugly memories.

This note was far different from the one he'd left for everyone to read that night. It also gave me the opening I needed. After I finished reading it, I handed the journal back to him. "I know this was private, Wyatt, but you should understand something. Something important."

His eyes teared up. "You're breaking up with me."

I nodded. "Sort of. In your note that night, you said I was the love of your life, but you never told me that. I really do love you, but not like you want."

He dropped onto the sofa, the book still in his hands.

"You're going for counseling, aren't you?"

He nodded. Now tears dripped down his face and dropped onto the cover of the book.

"I've been accepted at college. I'll be going away in the fall. Less than a month." When he didn't say anything, I wondered what to do next. What if he threatened to overdose again? "Do you want me to call your parents and ask them to come home early?

He shook his head. "Just go. You don't care any more than the others did. I thought you loved me."

"I told you. I do, but like a brother. I don't want to see you like this. Please, tell me you'll keep going to counseling."

"Just leave."

"Not until your father is here." I folded my arms and sat beside him. "Play your guitar."

He sniffled, but went and picked it up from its stand and began strumming. Before long he was lost in his music.

When his parents returned, I talked to his father, who reassured me he would take care of Wyatt. He thanked me for my concern and promised to keep me posted about Wyatt's recovery.

I left his house that night a sadder and wiser person. That didn't alter the fact that I would love him always and forever.

The End